Could a Tiger Be My Pet?

Written by:
Matt Reher

Illustrated by:
Drew Falchetta

BEWARE of CAT

How about a crocodile for a pet?
No one else has one, I bet.

But I won't think that
croc's so great
when she eats the meat
right off my plate.

Crocodiles have the strongest bite of any
animal. They mostly eat fish and birds, but they
could eat hippos, snakes, and even people.

3

No meat for giraffes – giraffes eat leaves.
They eat leaves right off the trees.

They eat all day, but when they're fed, giraffes won't fit inside my bed.

Giraffes sleep about 2 hours each day. They can sleep while they stand.

I'll take a blue whale for my pet.
I don't mind if my bed gets wet.

But a whale's the size of one long truck.
I think that means I'm out of luck.

A blue whale can grow up to 100 feet long.
It takes a lot of krill to feed this animal
– 40 million krill a day, in fact.

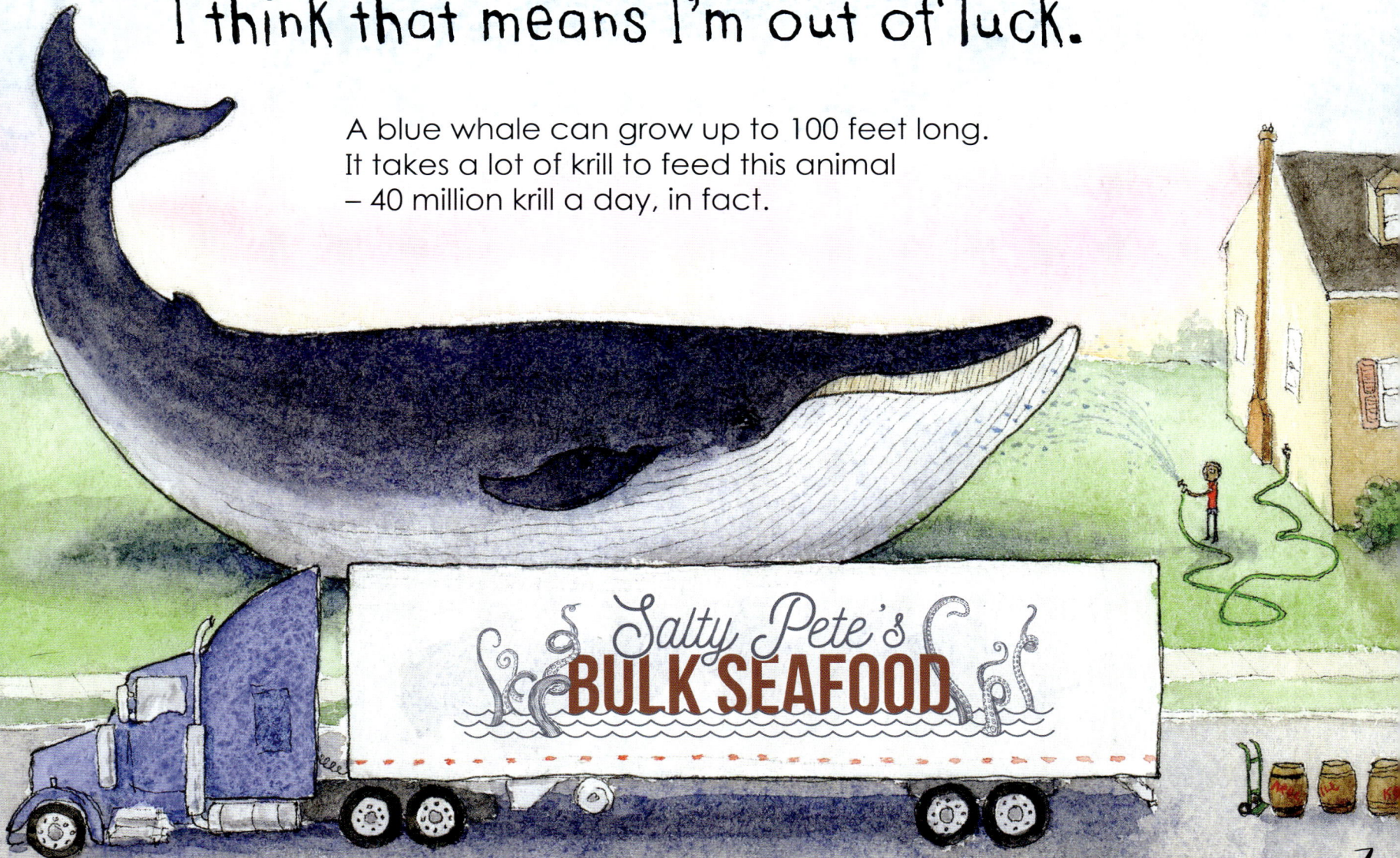

Salty Pete's
BULK SEAFOOD

A hummingbird - yes! I'd like to try.
They are small, and they can fly.

But those little wings are way too fast.
A pet like that would never last.

Hummingbirds can flap their wings 200 times in 1 second.
They can fly forward, backward, and upside down.

A caterpillar might do the trick.
They are small and not too quick.

This is a pet my friends should know. Hey! Where did my caterpillar go?

A caterpillar eats leaves for 2-3 weeks before making himself into a cocoon. About two weeks later, a butterfly comes out of this silky shell.

There are many pets that I could choose.
An elephant is one I'd never lose.

I'd always know when he's awake. But when he walks, the house would shake.

Elephants can grow up to 13 feet tall and weigh about 15,000 pounds!

An owl would not be such a pest.
An owl would live in its own nest.

Most Popular Pet Owl Name[ ]B...

Domestic Owls

The International Society of
Owl Owners & Trainers

OWLS: 101

Vol. III

Everything You Wanted to Know About Owls

SO YOU ADOPTED AN OWL - NOW WHAT?

HOW TO CARE FOR YOUR OWL
In Just 42 Easy Steps!

⑤

But when it came our time to play, the owl would sleep all through the day.

Most owls are nocturnal. This means they rest during the day and hunt for prey at night.

15

A beaver might eat all the chairs.

Beavers use the whole tree – some wood for eating and some wood for building dams.

Polar bears eat lots of seal blubber to get fat. This fat protects them from the Arctic cold.

My room's too hot for polar bears.

How about a tiger for my pet?

A tiger might be the best pet yet.

But all of these animals
live in the wild.
They can't live in a
house with a child.

Animals have slowly evolved,
or changed, over thousands
and thousands of years to be
able to survive in their homes.

They all need a place with lots of space to hunt and swim and fly and chase.

I want a pet that needs my care—
to give it food and brush its hair.

A dog!

A cat!

PET FOOD

D O G

CAT

A friend to pat.

They learn to love
girls and boys.
They'll lick my face
and play with toys.

Today, some animals are bred to
be friendly and live with people.
They grow to love their humans.

This is how our
story ends...

21

...come and meet my new best friends.

Use Words You Know
to read new words!

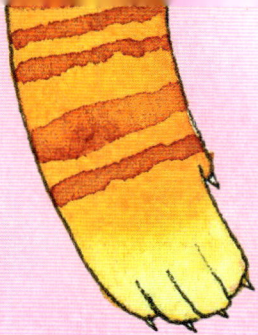

all	at	get	see
call	cat	yet	seed
mall	hat	wet	need
small	that	bet	feed
	pat	pet	feet
			meet

eat		play	
heat	not	day	make
meat	got	say	wake
mean	hot		shake

23

Tricky Words

always	never
friend	own
great	right
know	think
last	those
long	walk
mean	

About the Author Matt Reher

Matt has always dreamed of becoming a children's book author. Born in Iowa, raised in New Orleans, and now residing in Philadelphia, he enjoys music, cooking, and college football. Matt has a Bachelor of Arts degree in mass communication from Louisiana State University and a Master of Education degree from Chestnut Hill College. Matt spent many years as an elementary and high school teacher in Philadelphia and continues to work with schools and school districts around the country.

About the Illustrator Drew Falchetta

Drew likes to draw. This makes sense since his name is the past tense of draw. Drew has always drawn, but he attended the University of the Arts to study how to be a better drawer and painter. After receiving his Bachelor of Fine Arts degree in Illustration, Drew started drawing and painting for a living. For years, he illustrated for various freelance projects, greeting cards, and art galleries. When Drew is not drawing or painting, he spends time with his daughter and dog.

For more practice at this level, please visit
www.americanreadingathome.com

CleanWatts

Green-e
Energy
CERTIFIED

Printed with 100% renewable energy from mixed resources and low VOC vegetable-based inks

1-63437-448-7
978-1-63437-448-4